W9-AJT-287

J
359.83
Ra

$13.95
Rawlinson, Jonathan
    Hunter-killer
submarines

DATE DUE

MR 8'91	JUL 7 '00		
JE 24 91	JUL 05 95		
NO 14 91	DEC 29 95		
NO 29'91	JUL 23 96		
JE 17'92	MAY 24 '97		
JY 6'92	AUG 20 98		
DE 1 92	MR 30 99		
MR 15'92	JE 02 '04		
JY 1'93	DE 2 1 '00		
JY 22'93			
AG 11'93			
JN 9 '04			

EAU CLAIRE DISTRICT LIBRARY

DEMCO

The Sea Power Library

HUNTER-KILLER
SUBMARINES

The Sea Power Library

HUNTER-KILLER SUBMARINES

by Jonathan Rawlinson

Rourke Publications, Inc.
Vero Beach, Florida 32964

EAU CLAIRE DISTRICT LIBRARY

A nuclear-powered attack submarine of the Los Angeles class, the City of Corpus Christi creates a strong wake as it pushes through the sea at speed.

79728

Media Source 12/3/90 #/385

© 1989 Rourke Publications, Inc.

All rights reserved. No part of this book may be reproduced or utilized in any form or by any means, electronic or mechanical including photocopying, recording or by any information storage and retrieval system without permission in writing from the publisher.

Library of Congress Cataloging-in-Publication Data
Rawlinson, Jonathan, 1944-
　　Hunter-killer submarines/by Jonathan Rawlinson.
　　p. cm. — (The Sea power library)
　　Includes index.
　　Summary: Describes the history, development, uses, and capabilities of different types of submarines that patrol and guard American and Soviet sea lanes.
　　ISBN 0-86625-086-7
　　1. United States. Navy — Submarine forces — Juvenile literature.
[1. Submarines. 2. United States. Navy — Submarine forces.
3. Warships.] I. Title. II. Series.
V858.R38　1989　　　　　　　　　　88-31527
359.83 - dc19　　　　　　　　　　　　　CIP
　　　　　　　　　　　　　　　　　　　　　AC

Contents

What Is A Submarine?

The submarine is one of the most remarkable boats ever designed and built. It has probably the largest set of tasks ever given to a fighting ship. Most warship types have been developed quite recently and do not have a long history. The battleship and the frigate have origins that go back more than a hundred years. The cruiser was first used as recently as the late nineteenth century, and the destroyer is a comparatively modern warship. The aircraft carrier really came into its own only during the 1930s. The submarine, though, is more than 200 years old.

The submarine is one of the most remarkable ships ever built and carries out a very wide range of roles and duties in the modern navy.

Submarines like the Nathan Hale *were designed to carry long-range nuclear missiles to attack cities and land targets.*

Other submarines, like the one seen here, are built for attacking ships at sea.

7

Space is always at a premium aboard ships at sea, but never more so than in the cramped quarters of the modern submarine.

In 1776, during the Revolutionary War, Sergeant Ezra Lee took command of the submarine *Turtle* as it set out on a mission to seek and destroy the British flagship **HMS** *Eagle*. This action was the first modestly successful attempt at submarine warfare. The British warship was not destroyed, but the submarine did get underneath the *Eagle* and escaped without loss of life. The *Turtle* showed the enormous potential of the submarine, and engineers were encouraged to work on the tough problems that had to be overcome.

For several hundred years brave men had tried in vain to build machines that could carry them underwater. It was the ideal place from which to fight a war. Unseen, submarines could creep up on the enemy and sink them without danger of being fired upon. Some people said it was an unfair form of war and that it lacked the sporting chance of combat. They said submarines should be banned. But the potential advantages were too great, and men continued to work on submarine designs. It took a long time to develop the submarine into the boat we know today, although the basic technology existed more than 100 years ago.

One of the first successful designs was the French boat *Gymnote*, which appeared in 1888 with **electric propulsion**. This proved that submarines were a workable proposition. The *Gymnote* operated on the same basic principles that govern submarines today. It was generally cylindrical in shape and looked like a torpedo. This shape helped it slip smoothly through the water. The *Gymnote* consisted of two cylinders, one inside the other. In the space between the two hulls were tanks which, when filled with water, caused the submarine to sink in a controlled manner. All submarines today operate on this principle. To rise again, water was pumped out of the tanks, and they were filled with air. Today, submarines have fins and rudders to maintain control in their near silent movement through the seas.

Power for the *Gymnote* came from batteries, but in 1900 the French boat *Narval* carried a steam engine to propel it along on the surface. This gave it greater range on the surface and allowed it to operate over

Unlike surface boats, submarines provide little or no opportunity for going up on deck to gain relief from the confined quarters.

Submarines are able to operate in areas where no other ships can go, such as under the ice of the Arctic Ocean.

Like planes in the air, a submarine's path is controlled by the up and down movement of control surfaces seen here on each side of the sail.

A potent threat to underwater boats, this Lockheed P-3 Orion cruises past a fast-moving submarine.

larger areas of sea and ocean. Also in 1900, the American boat *Holland* pioneered the use of a gasoline engine, but this design had a major drawback. Vapor from the gasoline could create an explosive mixture which, if detonated, would blow the boat apart. In 1904, the French found a workable solution when the *Aigrette* appeared with a diesel motor. Diesel oil is much less volatile than gasoline, and diesel engines eventually ushered in the age of the modern submarine.

When war broke out in Europe in August 1914, the British used submarines to sink iron ore boats heading for Germany through the Baltic Sea. The Germans began to use submarines to attack merchant shipping in the Atlantic, and in May 1915 a German submarine sank the liner *Lusitania*, killing many innocent people. Once again, people called for the abolition of the submarine, but its usefulness in war had become too great for that to happen. European countries, and soon America too, were fighting to halt German attacks in central Europe, and no country was willing to ban any form of weapon that might help to win the war. When the war was over, the submarine was fully established as a major addition to naval forces.

When World War Two began in 1939, the German navy had 58 submarines, called **U-boats** from the German word *Unterseeboote,* which means under-sea boats. Between the two great wars, the submarine had been fully developed into a modern warship. The Japanese built giant cruiser-submarines to patrol the Pacific Ocean, while American submarines concentrated on long range endurance, crew comfort, and good handling. At the peak of German naval activity in the Atlantic Ocean, the U-boats were sinking ships faster than they could be built. The submarine was a crippling weapon of enormous devastation, and countries everywhere ignored it at their peril.

Whether delivered by air, surface ship, or another submarine, the torpedo is a constant threat.

Today, there are more submarines in service with the world's two major naval powers than any other class of warship. The Soviet Union operates about 385 submarines of many different types, although 60 of these are held in reserve. They would not be immediately available for war. The U.S. operates 146 submarines, but other **NATO** countries in Europe provide their own submarines to help patrol and guard the vital sea lanes that carry trade to and from America.

Submarine Duties

Submarines are unique in being able to dominate the vast ocean depths where no other ship can go. Because of that, the submarine is given tasks to do that range from general patrol duties to serving in all-out nuclear war. They are the most powerful boats ever built, capable of great destruction over enormous distances. Since 1963 one class of submarine has carried nuclear-tipped missiles, which form part of the strategic defense of the United States.

Each of these submarines carries 16 missiles; they began with Polaris missiles, and then came Poseidon. Each missile has greater explosive power than all the explosives used in World War One and World War Two combined. The latest generation of ballistic-missile submarines belong to the Ohio class, and each one has 20 Trident missiles with a range of 4,350 miles. Each missile carries about 10 warheads, and the Mark 2 Trident can fly 6,000 miles to its target. Each submarine, therefore, has the capacity to hit 200 separate targets with nuclear warheads.

The Sturgeon was the first boat in its class; 37 were built between 1963 and 1975 and each was powered by a water-cooled nuclear reactor, giving it an underwater speed of more than 30 knots.

In cost, ballistic-missile submarines are second only to giant nuclear-powered aircraft carriers. Each Ohio submarine costs about $1,500 million to build, and the 24 missiles it carries cost an additional $1,700 million. When each Ohio puts to sea on patrol, it represents $3,200 million in equipment and weapons! The U.S. Navy currently has 9 Ohio submarines in service and would like to increase this number to 24.

Ohio submarines are 560 feet long and have a submerged **displacement** of 18,700 tons. The largest submarine in the world is the Soviet's biggest ballistic-missile submarine, which has a submerged displacement of 25,000 tons. These are giant boats with enormous firepower. At the other end of the scale are small submarines, which are just as important but do different jobs.

The ballistic-missile submarine is designed to hide and to remain hidden for as long as possible. It is built to serve as a submerged missile launching pad and not to attack other submarines or surface ships. If found by the enemy it would be a crucial target to attack. Because of that, the navy knew it had to develop some form of protection for the missile boats.

Built by the Soviet Union, this Charlie I-class nuclear-attack submarine has been leased to India.

Tugs and small boats gently nudge a submarine into its berthing position.

Submarines from the United States and Britain meet up at the North Pole.

Nuclear Hunters

Modern SSBN Force Levels

ARCTIC OCEAN   ARCTIC OCEAN

★ USSR
22 DELTA
11 YANKEE
4 TYPHOON

★ USSR
16 DELTA
9 YANKEE

US
7 OHIO ★

ATLANTIC OCEAN

★ US
30 LAFAYETTE
BEN. FRANKLIN

PACIFIC OCEAN

ATLANTIC OCEAN

INDIAN OCEAN

PACIFIC OCEAN

The development of advanced torpedoes made it possible to seek out enemy submarines that threatened merchant ships and submerged ballistic-missile submarines in wartime. During the late 1940s, the United States developed the role of the anti-submarine submarine. Before that, most submarines were built to attack and sink surface ships. Now, sub-surface warfare has become a powerful aspect of naval conflict.

Hunter-killer submarines are built to search out and destroy enemy targets. These targets can be surface ships or submerged submarines. The hunter-killers must be quiet, fast, reliable, and well armed. They must operate for long periods far from home to protect supplies coming in from a foreign country. Hunter-killers must attack other submarines that threaten the underwater missile boats, or destroy enemy surface raiders like cruisers or frigates. They must dive deep and carry powerful detection devices to "listen" for other submarines or ships.

Only five countries operate submarines capable of

The designation SSBN stands for Sub-Surface Ballistic Nuclear, indicating the class of submarine designed to carry long-range ballistic missiles with nuclear warheads.

Ballistic-missile boats carry their missiles in vertical ▶
tubes located aft of the sail.

attacking targets on land several thousand miles away with nuclear-tipped ballistic misiles. These are the United States, the Soviet Union, Britain, France, and China. Many other countries have hunter-killers vital for the protection of their surface fleets. Recently, these submarines have been given another duty: to attack surface ships with long-range missiles or land targets like docks, ports, harbors, and towns where military forces threaten.

For operating long periods underwater far from home, there is no better power system than **nuclear propulsion**. Unlike oil or diesel engines, nuclear-powered engines do not burn fuel to drive the turbines that turn the screws. This means that they can remain underwater far longer than boats that must come to the surface to refuel or take in supplies. Before the introduction of nuclear power, submarines had to spend a lot of time on the surface, where they were vulnerable to discovery and attack. Nuclear

Ohio *returns to port after a lengthy mission at sea.*

power plants give the submarine a dramatic and powerful capability.

The first production-line nuclear-powered submarine was the *Skate*, built during the second half of the 1950s. It followed closely the design of the **USS** *Nautilus*, which pioneered nuclear propulsion for sub-surface boats. The *Skate* had a maximum displacement of 2,500 tons and was 267 feet long.

Skate was the first submarine to make a completely submerged crossing of the Atlantic Ocean. This feat would have been impossible to perform with diesel-electric engines. In 1958, the *Skate* achieved what was then a record 31 days submerged without coming up for air. It also made a polar cruise and became the first submarine to surface at the North Pole.

Four Skate-class boats were built, but only *Swordfish* remains in service. This class was followed by the Skipjack boats. Six Skipjacks were built in the late 1950s and early 1960s. They were the first to have the now familiar tear-drop hull shape with **diving planes** relocated from the hull to the **sail**. The diving planes control the submarine as it submerges or

The latest U.S. ballistic-missile submarine is the Ohio class; each is capable of carrying 24 long-range missiles. ▶

Each Ohio-class boat is capable of remaining at sea for several months, submerged at a secret location and ready for operational duty should it ever be called upon to fire its missiles in anger.

surfaces, while the sail is the structure on top of the hull that carries the periscopes and a look-out point for the crew on the surface. The Skipjacks were a little shorter and fatter than the Skate class.

There are only four Skipjack submarines in service today, and they were followed by the Thresher class. The first boat, the USS *Thresher*, was lost with all 129 crew members when it sank off the New England coast in April 1963. After that tragic loss, the class was renamed for the second boat in the series, the USS *Permit*. These boats had the Skate's length and the Skipjack's breadth, with a maximum displacement of more than 4,200 tons.

The first U.S. ballistic-missile submarine was the ◄ *Lafayette, launched in 1962 and designed to carry 16 Polaris missiles.*

A nuclear-powered submarine is designed for maintenance-free operation at sea, but when it comes to port extensive inspection and sometimes repair is essential.

The navy still operates 13 Permit-class boats, each with four torpedo tubes and four launching tubes for Harpoon anti-ship missiles. These submarines have a greater diving capability than the earlier boats, and the last three had special modifications as a result of the inquiry into the loss of *Thresher*. Operational experience with the Permit class led the navy on to its next hunter-killer class, named after the USS *Sturgeon*. The Sturgeon class was based on lessons learned from the Permit boats, and the Sturgeons comprise the second biggest attack force in the navy.

The Sturgeon class was built for anti-submarine work and was basically an enlarged and improved Permit boat. It had a length of 292 feet and a displacement of 4,640 tons. Built between 1963 and 1975, the 37 Sturgeon-class boats are capable of diving to more than 1,300 feet and have a top submerged speed of more than 30 **knots**. They carry anti-submarine mines and torpedoes, and like Permit boats they each carry four Harpoon missiles.

Sturgeons are being converted to carry eight Tomahawk missiles in addition to their original weapons.

Some Sturgeon boats have been equipped with special electronic equipment to gather information about possible enemy activity. Some have made special trips close inside Soviet waters to spy on Russian warships and communication systems. On at least one occasion, a Sturgeon boat got stuck for several hours inside Soviet Far East seas when it ran aground in shallow water. Soviet submarines have been known to do the same thing trying to gather intelligence in foreign waters.

The enormous bulk of the Ohio-class boat is readily discernible here, with the **Michigan** *high and dry; its two rows of 12 missile launching tubes are clearly visible on top of the hull.*

Los Angeles Class

Taking the best of the Skipjack, Permit, and Sturgeon classes, the navy moved on during the early 1970s to plan what is today the most powerful hunter-killer submarine in service with the U.S. Navy. The class is called Los Angeles after the first in the series, completed in 1976. The boats in the Skipjack class were known for their good speed in the water. The Permit and the Sturgeon submarines have very good anti-submarine detectors and weapons capability. The Los Angeles class has all these features and more.

The USS *Los Angeles* took four years to build. Before it was even launched, 13 more submarines of this type were under construction. By the end of 1988, the navy had 43 operational Los Angeles-class submarines. Of these, 13 operate in the Pacific Ocean and 30 in the Atlantic Ocean. The 37 Sturgeon-class submarines and the 43 Los Angeles-class

Nuclear-powered, but designed for a very different role than ballistic-missile submarines, the Corpus Christi *pushes on through a heavy sea.*

submarines make up the majority of America's naval hunter-killer boats.

Los Angeles boats are 360 feet long, have a beam of 33 feet, and displace more than 6,900 tons submerged. They are about 50 percent bigger than the Sturgeon class, which were the biggest hunter-killers in the U.S. Navy before the Los Angeles class was developed. Los Angeles boats are capable of diving more than 1,400 feet beneath the surface and moving underwater at a maximum speed of more than 30 knots.

Sailors aboard the Los Angeles-class boat, La Jolla, monitor critical instruments and displays that report the condition of every part of the submarine.

Attack submarines of the Los Angeles class are
▲ designed to seek and destroy enemy ships or
submarines in the event of war.

Los Angeles boats bristle with complex sensors and
equipment designed to detect and identify friendly or
enemy forces on the surface or under the sea. ▼

Each boat carries approximately 133 officers and men and weapons capable of a wide variety of duties. The submarines can lay mines, fire torpedoes, launch rockets, or send off **cruise missiles** to attack other ships or land targets. When first deployed with the navy, Los Angeles submarines could not carry cruise missiles, but modifications are being made so they can carry the Tomahawk.

Los Angeles boats are the first U.S. Navy submarines to have the speed to keep up with aircraft carriers. They provide a useful service as escort for these giant surface ships. Yet they are not the fastest submarines afloat. The Soviet Alpha class are capable of a top underwater speed of around 45 knots. On one occasion, an Alpha boat easily outran a trailing Los Angeles boat by putting on a burst of speed. Los Angeles boats are, however, good at trailing other types of Soviet submarines.

With advanced and sophisticated electronic search equipment, the Los Angeles boats have a good track record when it comes to finding Soviet boats and stalking them unobserved. In one instance,

The Birmingham leaps to the surface in a dramatic escape from the deep.

the captain of a Los Angeles boat successfully kept up with and tracked the course of two Soviet Delta submarines. He did this for a long period of time; in wartime those Delta submarines would be vulnerable to the superior electronics and technology of the Los Angeles boats.

Submarines like these are not cheap. In 1989, a single Los Angeles submarine costs about $700 million. The navy wants to buy a large number of these submarines because it thinks that, despite the cost, they are good value for the money. Attack submarines like those in the Los Angeles class would help keep enemy submarines away from merchant ships and other surface boats. This class of warship will last for a very long time into the future, because nothing can replace them and do the same job. That is why the navy hopes to buy at least 23 more Los Angeles boats, bringing the total to 66.

Boats of the Los Angeles class carry mines, ◄ tube-launched torpedoes, and missiles such as Tomahawk and Harpoon.

Los Angeles attack submarines carry a crew of more than 130 officers and enlisted men and can operate below the surface at a speed of more than 30 knots.

Beyond the Los Angeles class, submarine designers are working on the Seawolf class. The navy says they will be "the fastest, deepest diving, most heavily armed United States submarines ever put to sea." Seawolf will be slightly shorter than the Los Angeles class and have a length of about 350 feet with a beam of 40 feet. It will be fatter than Los Angeles and displace 9,150 tons submerged, about 30 percent more than the Los Angeles boats.

Seawolf is expected to have a submerged top speed of more than 35 knots, enabling it to keep up with the Soviet Sierra-class submarine. It will have a very advanced nuclear reactor and have the capacity to remain submerged for long periods. Submarines in the Seawolf class are not expected to appear in operational service before the mid-1990s.

Modern Diesel Submarines

The modern submarine is a far cry from the diesel-powered boats operated just a few decades ago, such as Grayback.

Of the 146 submarines currently operated by the U.S. Navy, 38 are designed to hide under the sea and launch powerful ballistic missiles in wartime. In addition, the navy has 103 nuclear-powered attack submarines and 5 powered by diesel engines. The nuclear-powered submarines are quieter than the diesels and provide much greater range and endurance, because they can operate away from port far longer than oil-fired boats.

Whether nuclear-powered or diesel-powered, life aboard a submarine can be hours of endless boredom.

The oldest operational submarine in service with the U.S. Navy is the *Darter*, built between 1954 and 1956. For the past 10 years it has operated from a base in Japan. It is 284 feet long, carries a crew of 93, and has a submerged displacement of 2,300 tons. Only slightly newer are the three Barbel-class submarines, 219 feet long with a displacement of 2,900 tons.

Darter and the Barbel-class submarines were the last of the diesel-electric boats built for the navy. They carry only torpedo tubes for armament and although they play a support role they would never be assigned a major mission in wartime.

One other submarine is of interest. Built between 1962 and 1968, the USS *Dolphin* is a deep-diving research boat able to carry out scientific studies of the ocean. It is also used for **sonar** research into different methods of detecting other boats above or below the surface. The *Dolphin* is 152 feet long and carries 37 crew members and up to 7 scientists.

*Typical of the Barbel-class diesel-electric submarine is the **Bonefish**, built in 1958.*

Weapons

Boosted into the air by a rocket motor, a Tomahawk cruise missile is fired by a submarine toward some distant target on land.

Targets to attack are usually designated by computers and electronic equipment; the submarine crew rarely gets the chance to see what their weapons are aimed at.

For many years the only weapon available to the attack submarine was the torpedo fired through several tubes installed in the forward hull. Sometimes a fixed gun was mounted on deck to protect the boat from attack by air or from fast surface raiders. Now, with the development of missiles for almost every application, submarines are equipped with weapons able to hit targets up to 1,600 miles away.

The navy uses the McDonnell Douglas Harpoon missile in fast attack submarines. With a range of up to 100 miles, the missile is fired from a tube launcher on the submarine. This missile is the latest development in the Harpoon family of air- and ship-launched missiles. Harpoon flies to its target propelled by a small jet engine and achieves a maximum speed of 640 MPH.

Working on the same principle as Harpoon, the General Dynamics Tomahawk is capable of flying to a target over 1,600 miles away from a rocket-boosted underwater launch. Tomahawk is pushed to the surface by compressed gas, much like a cork is pushed out the neck of a bottle. When it clears the surface, a small rocket motor ignites to accelerate the missile up and away. A few seconds later the motor burns out, and the case drops away. A small jet engine is started to propel the missile through the air.

At 525 MPH it may take three hours for Tomahawk to reach its target. The missile has extremely accurate guidance equipment and at maximum range the margin of error is measured in just a few feet! Both Harpoon and Tomahawk can be fitted with conventional high-explosive or nuclear warheads and either missile can be used against surface or land targets.

For attacking other submarines, the **SUBROC** (submarine rocket) has been widely used by the navy. Launched through a torpedo tube, its powerful rocket blasts it out of the water and powers it for a flight of up

Other missiles are carried for different reasons; here the launch tubes for ballistic missiles are lined up along the center of the submarine's hull.

to 35 miles before it drops a nuclear depth charge. A depth charge is a bomb designed to explode below the surface at a pre-set depth. SUBROC is 22 feet long and weighs 2 tons. It has a maximum speed of about 1,100 MPH and its nuclear charge will destroy any submarine within a range of four miles.

For the 1990s, the navy will begin using the Sea Lance missile, which is expected to have a range of up to 100 miles. Sea Lance will be primarily fitted to the Los Angeles-class submarine. With this missile, the submarine will be in a position to protect fast-moving aircraft carrier battle groups from attack by enemy submarines.

Submarines are also used to lay mines in heavily defended waters or inshore areas where surface ships would come under fire. The mines they lay are about 13 feet long, 19 inches in diameter and weigh 1,660 pounds. The standard anti-submarine torpedo is the Mark 48, just over 19 feet long with a diameter of 21 inches and a weight of 3,480 pounds. The Mark 48 has a top speed of 60 knots and a range of 23 miles.

In a test carried out in 1986, a Tomahawk cruise missile launched from a submerged submarine approached its target after a flight of more than 400 miles.

Operating completely on coded instructions from its programmed computer, Tomahawk detonated its 1,000-pound warhead directly over the simulated airfield after flying more than 400 miles.

Soviet Submarines

The Soviet submarine fleet is by far the largest in the world and operates some of the most advanced boats built. At the end of 1988, the Soviet navy had around 385 submarines in operation, with an additional 60 in reserve at ports and docks. Of the total, 74 are ballistic-missile launching submarines and 311 are attack submarines. Some are very old and have been around since the 1950s. Others are new and extremely well designed.

The Soviets operate more than 130 nuclear-powered attack submarines in 12 separate classes (Echo, Charlie, Oscar, Papa, Victor, Alpha, Mike, Sierra, Akula, November, Yankee, and Hotel). The 23 boats in the November, Yankee, and Hotel classes were built and first operated as ballistic-missile submarines. When new submarines were added to the fleet, the total number of boats exceeded the international arms limit on boats of that type. The Soviets then converted those 23 boats to the attack role.

Built during the 1960s, the Soviet Juliett-class diesel-electric attack submarine carries a crew of 79 and has a maximum speed of 12 knots.

The comparatively modern Kilo class is a relatively small patrol boat, carrying a crew of 45 and possessing a maximum dived speed of no more than 25 knots.

In addition to the nuclear-powered submarines, the Soviet navy operates more than 150 diesel-powered submarines in six separate classes (Whiskey, Romeo, Foxtrot, Tango, Kilo and Juliett). Of the total submarine force, about 90 operate in the Pacific Ocean, with the rest operating in what the Soviets call "northern water," which means the North Atlantic Ocean, the Baltic Sea, and the Barents Sea.

The biggest attack submarines in the world belong to the nuclear-powered Oscar class. Each boat is 492 feet long with a hull 60 feet wide and 36 feet deep. These massive boats displace 16,000 tons submerged and carry 130 sailors. Oscar is capable of firing 24 supersonic missiles, each with a maximum range of more than 300 miles. The missiles are kept in tubes located in a 10-foot gap between an inner and an outer hull. The double hull also helps protect the submarine's machinery from attack.

The fastest submarines are the six Alpha-class boats, with a top speed of 45 knots. They are also the deepest diving boats, capable of going down more than 2,500 feet. Some experts say they have an emergency maximum diving depth of almost 4,000 feet. In theory, the deeper submarines go, the safer they are because few weapons can go down that far.

The most commonly used Soviet submarines are the 44 Victor and 45 Whiskey-class boats. Nuclear-powered Victor-class boats displace around 6,000 tons and can be used for laying mines,

▲
With a dived speed of 45 knots, the Alpha nuclear-fleet defense submarine is one of the fastest in the world.

With a displacement of 8,000 tons, the nuclear-powered Akula class has a speed of more than 42 knots; it first ▶ *appeared in 1984.*

The Oscar-class cruise-missile submarines have a displacement of more than 16,000 tons, a crew of 130, and ▶ *two pressurized water reactors that propel it to a dived speed of more than 35 knots.*

186 YDS OR 170M

120 YDS OR 110M

27 YDS OR 25M

53 1/3 YDS OR 49M

10 20 30 40 50 40 30 20 10

Football Field

Oscar-class boats are equipped with 24 supersonic missiles, each with a range of 340 miles.

Largest ever built, Typhoon-class submarines each ◀ carry 20 long-range ballistic nuclear missiles and are longer than a football field.

attacking other submarines, or going after surface ships. The diesel-powered Whiskey boats are among the oldest submarines in service. They were all built during the 1950s and have little real value in a modern war. They are noisy and easily detected and, compared to nuclear-powered submarines, perform poorly.

Whiskey-class submarines are 249 feet long and displace 1,350 tons with a crew of 54. In addition to 45 operational boats, the Soviets hold 60 Whiskey boats in reserve. More than half the Soviet submarine force is old. Recently, the Soviets have been building very modern, heavily armed submarines for ocean patrols. It will not be long before the older Soviet submarines are replaced with large numbers of these boats.

In the past the Soviets have concentrated on the use of submarines for home defense. They began replacing World War Two submarines by introducing different designs for three lines of defense. In 1948, under their leader, Joseph Stalin, they planned to

Typhoon ballistic-missile submarines are designed to be re-loaded with new missiles at sea.

build 1,200 submarines. About 200 would have been built for long-range duty; these were the Zulu and Foxtrot classes. The medium-range defense was to be the responsibility of 900 Whiskey and Romeo boats. The inner defenses were to be controlled by 100 boats of the Quebec class.

This ambitious plan was modified when nuclear propulsion came along. Less than 370 diesel submarines were actually built, and under half remain in use today. Nuclear boats were more expensive to build, and the development of missile technology added new roles for submarines. These included attacks on ships beyond the horizon, the use of nuclear depth charges against other submarines, and attacks on land targets from a submerged position.

The diesel-powered Kilo-class patrol submarine is the latest Soviet design for home defense duties. It is 230 feet long and carries 45 crew members at a top speed of 25 knots. It has a displacement of 3,200 tons and eight torpedo tubes in the forward hull. These

boats are believed to specialize in laying mines.

Larger than patrol submarines, nuclear-powered fleet submarines are capable of attacking land targets with long-range missiles. The **SS-N-**21 missile can be launched from the torpedo tube of a submerged submarine. After reaching the surface and taking to the air, the SS-N-21 can reach targets 1,600 miles away. In this regard the Soviet fleet submarines are the equivalent of America's Permit, Sturgeon, and Los Angeles submarines.

The latest Soviet fleet submarines are the Sierra and Akula classes. Sierra is 360 feet long and has a displacement of 7,600 tons. It can fire long-range missiles and torpedoes or carry up to 60 mines. By the late 1980s, only two Sierra boats were in service, but many more are expected to be built. The Akula-class submarines are each 351 feet in length with a displacement of 8,000 tons. They are quite similar to Sierra but can travel at a higher speed (42 knots) and have a larger store of weapons.

The Soviets have split their submarine forces between nuclear and diesel-electric propulsion to a much greater extent than the United States. The Soviets continue to build diesel submarines, while the U.S. has only five left in service. The Soviet policy is to balance expensive but technically advanced boats with cheaper, less capable boats to provide large numbers for the defense of home waters. The Soviets use the nuclear submarines for long-range ocean patrols. The diesel boats carry out duties where range and endurance is not necessary.

Soviet submarines routinely operate in all the major oceans of the world.

Primary Soviet Submarine Deployment Areas 1984

ARCTIC OCEAN

ARCTIC OCEAN

ATLANTIC OCEAN

PACIFIC OCEAN

ATLANTIC OCEAN

INDIAN OCEAN

PACIFIC OCEAN

Includes all operational
Soviet submarines

Anti-Submarine Forces

Submarines are difficult to detect because they operate in vast open waters of the world's seas and oceans. The most effective way to find a submarine is to use an echo-sounder, or sonar detector. It works by sending a sound signal through the water, much like a radio speaker sends out sound waves in an air-filled room. When the sound signal strikes something solid it bounces back. This reflected sound is picked up by the ship that broadcast the signal. It is called "active" sonar because the surface ship has to send out a series of sound signals to get reflected information back.

By carefully designing equipment to recognize different shapes and objects in the water, operators can tell whether the reflected sound has bounced off a whale, a shoal of fish, or a submarine. With modern equipment, sonar can provide information about the distance to the object, its size, and what speed it is moving at. If a surface ship finds a submarine, it can then track it and select weapons to destroy it.

One drawback with active sonar is that it can be detected by submarines. If a submarine crew picks up sonar signals coming its way, it will know that a

Built to operate from aircraft carriers at sea, the Lockheed S-3B Viking carries sophisticated sensors and complex anti-submarine warfare kit, including weapons with which it can destroy ships.

Helicopters like the MH-53E play a vital part in helping to clear mines, possibly laid by enemy submarines, from the sea lanes.

surface ship is hunting for it. The submarine may escape, hide on the seabed, or attack the surface ship first. For that reason, some ships now use "passive" sonar. Passive sonar puts listening devices in the water to pick up the rumbling sound of a submarine engine.

It is not easy to keep a submarine quiet. Water conducts sound well, and even the movement of water around a boat as it moves forward sends out disturbances that can be picked up. Sound detectors that merely sit in the water and listen for noise are called **hydrophones.**

Ships tow lines of hydrophones through the water, passively listening for submarines. Aircraft and helicopters drop hydrophones that carry small transmitters to radio the information to the plane. The aircraft operating on this duty carry weapons to attack the submarines. Sometimes, hydrophones are attached to the sea floor in very long strings to cover enormous areas. These routinely keep track of submarines going over them.

Other forms of submarine detection are more technically advanced. Submarines moving slowly through the water far below the surface generate a wake just as ships on the surface do. Eventually, the submarine's wake reaches the surface and leaves a tell-tale trail. The trail is not nearly as apparent as the wake from a surface ship, but it is sufficient for advanced measuring equipment to identify the existence of a submarine.

Both the United States and the Soviet Union are experimenting with radars that observe the surface of the ocean over great distances, far beyond the horizon. They hope to develop equipment that can observe minute changes in the wave pattern and report the hidden location of submarines. Satellites can now measure the slight rise of a few inches in water level when a submarine slips through the sea, and this method may also help detect submarines. However sophisticated the science of anti-submarine warfare becomes, though, the undersea warship is likely to have a very long life ahead.

Probably the world's most effective shore-based anti-submarine warfare plane, the Lockheed P-3C Orion carries sophisticated surveillance equipment and large quantities of weapons. ▼

Surface ships seek out and attempt to identify the precise location of submarines at sea, so that if war should break out they can be ready to attack.

Although historically considered the submarine's primary weapon, torpedoes launched by surface ships or aircraft are still a major threat to underwater boats.

Abbreviations

HMS   Her Majesty's Ship

NATO   North Atlantic Treaty Organization

An alliance of the U.S., Canada, and 11 West European countries operating under a military pact to support one another; an attack on one is considered an attack on all.

SUBROC   Submarine Rocket

A rocket launched through a torpedo tube capable of carrying a conventional or nuclear warhead to a target on the surface of the sea or on land.

USS   United States Ship

Designation for a warship of the United States Navy, such as *USS Bronstein*.

Glossary

Cruise missiles — Small pilotless flying bombs usually propelled to their targets by a small turbojet engine.

Displacement — The measure of the size of a ship, given by the amount of water it displaces. Figures given in this book are for full-load displacement, when the ship is fully armed, equipped, and loaded for war.

Diving planes — Small control surfaces, or flaps, attached to the side of the submarine which control its direction or movement in the water.

Electric propulsion — Battery-powered electric motors that drive propeller shafts for propulsion.

Hunter-killer submarines — Submarines built to search out and destroy enemy targets on the surface or underwater.

Hydrophones — Microphone-like sound detectors that rest in the water and listen for the noise of approaching ships or submarines.

Knot — The measure of speed at sea.
1 knot = 1 nautical mile per hour.

Nuclear propulsion — A form of propulsion in which heat from a nuclear reactor drives steam turbines attached to a propeller shaft.

Sail — The structure on top of a submarine helm that carries periscopes and a look-out point for the crew when the vessel is on the surface.

Sonar — SOund, NAvigation and Ranging. A device using sound waves to detect submerged submarines.

U-boat — The common name given to German submarines derived from the German word for underwater boats.

Index

Page references in *italics* indicate photographs or illustrations.